Trump's Triumph

The Drumbeats of World War III...

To know how we got here,
Read: The Road to World War III: Can the Dark Forces of anti-Freedom Trump Humanity?

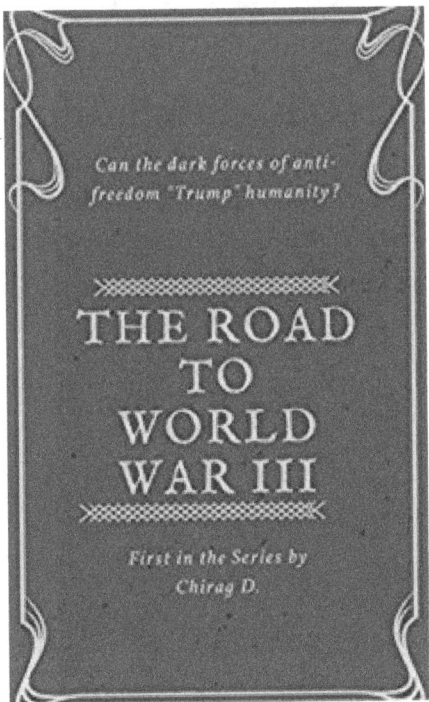

Contents

Preface

Nov 9, 2016. Early morning, as the final results came in, angry protests spill onto the streets across various cities in the United States chanting slogans against Donald Trump. How did a political outsider, who the liberals claim had made racist, sexist, misogynist, homophobic and anti-Islamic comments with regularity, win the White House? This is the book about the inside story of how that happened.

People inside and outside of the US are still reeling from the shock of Donald Trump's astounding victory in the US Presidential elections. America's adversaries and allies are equally surprised by this event. Were people so disenchanted with the political system that Hillary Clinton represented?

A tide of discontented White Americans swept Trump into the White House in a historic election. So called it "White-lash" against a Black President. So termed it as hatred against a woman candidate. The voters clearly wanted to send a message to the political establishment: You Are Fired!

Trump supporters claimed they felt overlooked by the political elites. For years they have been ignored by both the major political parties. As globalization raged on, middle America got buried under the intense pressure of competition and cheap foreign labor.

The numbers are startling. Nearly 60% of all Whites voted for Donald Trump, including a majority of white women. The claims of women being offended by Trump falls flat in front of this statistic. It wasn't just older voters. 5% more whites under the age of 29 voted for Trump compared to Hillary. Furthermore, more than half (55%) of white college graduates voted for Trump over Hillary. They were all willing to overlook Trump's comments about Mexicans and Muslims.

Liberals are so stunned by the results that some have called for introspection on America's national character!

This election divided America into two separate moral universe. The things that are considered acceptable by both the groups are distinctly different. The book is a study of what are they and where it will lead America and the world. The book concludes that we are in the initial stages of World War III, a global military conflict of epic proportions, being fought between ideologies that overlap religion, economic systems and political culture.

Introduction

Dec 29, 2016. As threatened, Obama unveils new sanctions against Russia over election hacking allegations. Despite president-elect Trump's reservations, the sanctions also including the expulsion of 35 Russian diplomats and closing of two Russian compounds in New York and Maryland.

The Russian diplomats would have 72 hours to leave the United States.

Jan 4, 2017. Following the horrific New Year's Day attack on an Istanbul nightclub which left 39 people dead, Turkish jets carry out a number of airstrikes against suspected ISIS group positions in Syria.

2016 was another game-changing for WikiLeaks, the whistleblowing site, as it delivered a massive trove of documents over the 12-month period. These included over 50,000 emails. The emails relating to the US election rocked the Democratic establishment and delivered a blow to the Clinton campaign in the lead-up to the November election.

As President-elect Donald Trump continues to surprise the world with his new appointments in key positions, the world is certainly moving toward the completion of the Trilogy that started, remember, when an Austrian archduke was assassinated by Austrians of Slav origin, who had their loyalties with Serbia!

Trump team is also proposing a 10% import tariff on all goods coming into the United States from China. The first shot in the trade war? Geopolitics is coming a full circle. Russia which was an indirect ally of the United States in the second world war, is now once again looking at America and her new President with friendly eyes.

Obama legacy looks to be drowning as Trump has vowed to reverse Obama's every executive action. Far Right parties are sweeping polls, from Australia to America to the heartland of Europe. Every other day, Europe is suffering from terror attacks, either in the form of mass murder like the

Berlin Christmas market bus crash, or the frequent molestation of European women at the hands of refugees.

If civil war breaks out in Europe, as feared by the French President, the situation will truly be of an explosive kind.

Latin American & African countries are especially vulnerable to currency failures, as we are witnessing in Argentina. It will only aid China, which is preparing to capitalize on their misery; and Islamists who are busy setting up base in South America.

DoS (Denial of Service) attacks, a type of large scale cyber warfare, that temporarily blacked out the whole Internet were witnessed by the entire world recently. Then there was China's attempt to steal American military secrets using cyber attacks on the Pentagon. Chaos seems to be the only constant going forward.

If there is one country that qualifies for the title of lunatics, it has to be North Korea. China uses the small nation as its pawn against South Korea, and increasingly against Japan. In the coming years, it is quite possible that China uses North Korea to wage a war with South Korea, a US ally. 20,000 US soldiers are stationed in South Korea. China does not like their presence so close to their homeland one bit.

With the assassination of the Russian ambassador in Ankara, Turkey has openly crossed swords with the Russian bear. Putin will have his revenge. In the meantime, Turkey, a relatively moderate Muslim nation is turning radical at an alarming pace. Will Turkey be the gateway to Europe for Jihadis from Syria? Is the border between Turkey and Greece/Bulgaria the new "Gates of Vienna"?

A Jewish nation surrounded by Arab enemies, fighting for survival since formation. Israel has the distinction of defeating 6 Arab armies simultaneously while capturing additional territory in the process! In the ongoing WW3, Israel is playing a crucial role. On one hand Israel funds Sunni terror groups like ISIS to counterbalance Shia fanaticism sponsored by Iran. Meanwhile, the nation has a deep influence on American politics.

The Israel Lobby in the US will play a pivotal role in the ever-changing equations in the middle east and beyond.

Interesting to note that while Russia is campaigning against ISIS, the very group Israel covertly buys oil from, Israel-Russia relations have never been better.

As Islamic Jihad becomes increasingly more powerful, partly due to the Western world's political correctness and partly because the sheer desperation of Jihadists, terrorist attacks across the democratic world are expected to rise exponentially.

Fuelled by Saudi Arabia, the Sunni terror groups may launch a direct attack on Shia Iran, shedding any pretense of diplomacy or restraint.

Remember that Saudi Arabia is finding in extremely tough to balance the budget due to low oil price. One way of boosting the oil price is by fuelling war in the region. Int is estimated the Saudi Kingdom may go bankrupt by 2020. They need an oil price higher than $105 to break even on their oil production. Anything less is a deficit for the Kingdom.

One of the biggest enemies of Saudi oil, is US Shale. As the international crude price rises, it becomes more profitable to extract Shale in America. This has a dampening effect on oil price which in turn hurts Saudis. Shale innovates to stay profitable at a lower oil price but Saudis cant. If Saudi government defaults, the Kingdom may break into two, with factions openly going against US interests.

Third World War is the reality we are living through, which can be described by the phrase, "The Perfect Storm". It is a military conflict on a global scale and at different levels. It has many dimensions like Economic, Social, Religious, Geopolitical and Ideological. The three trends shaping WW3 are: 1) The rise of Jihad in the middle-east & beyond; 2) China's military expansion & modernization; 3) The economic de-leveraging of the western world.

The above 3 trends could be approximately mapped on a timeline in phases as follows:
1) 2014-2018 (Incremental or rising violence phase)
2) 2018-2019 (Peak violence phase)
3) 2019-2025 (Decremental or rehabilitation phase)

The above 3 phases are characterized by the combined strength of the 3 trends noted earlier above. Meaning from 2014 to 2018-19, global violence will keep rising owing to all 3 trends gaining momentum. In this phase, Islamist Jihad will continue gaining strength. Partly because the West refuses to act against it due to political correctness, and partly because of Jihad owns inherent devilish characteristics. Phase-I will also witness Western world's continued de-leveraging (a downward economic spiral fueled by excessive debt. Combine this with China's rising military muscle.

Part I

Trump had never held political office, and he has now been elected the 45th President of the United States. He victory over Hillary Clinton is being termed as the biggest political upset in recent American history. Trump won big in rural areas but he also won the swing states of Ohio, Florida and Pennsylvania. Trump's win ends two years of divisive campaigning from both candidates. His victory speech urged unity.

But the mainstream media didn't see this coming. Almost all polls saw a Clinton victory as a given.

Trump's triumph shows the businessman's ability to smash expectations. It also showed the depth of anger in the American electorate, against the established political structure. It's hard to quantify and analyse how much and from where this rage comes from, even the Republican Party was caught unaware of the phenomenon.

How much of Trump's support base is driven by the fear White people feel about losing the top spot in the racial hierarchy in America, and how much of it is economic paranoia given the lack of wage growth in the last 4 years.

Trump built his campaign in his own image: Blunt & Provocative. He attracted thousands upon thousands to his rallies across the country. The idea of a Trump Presidency rose out of the ashes of the Romney loss in the 2012 elections. Within weeks, Trump trademarked the "Make America Great Again" slogan!

His comments didn't matter. With every rally, his support base swelled, until it was impossible to accommodate the people in smaller venues. He began to rent out stadiums! The rhetoric only intensified. In the end of the primaries, he defeated 16 other Republican leaders, some of them career politicians. He was now impossible to ignore.

Trump promised to return America to her greatness. A term that meant something different to everyone. For some, it was about revitalizing the failing US economy. To others, it was about military superiority. Whatever it was, the result for Trump was the same. More votes at the ballot!

The Ruling Elite Is Protected From The Consequences Of Its Dominance

There are many sources of rage: injustice, the destruction of truth, powerlessness. But if we had to identify the one key source of non-elite rage that cuts across all age, ethnicity, gender, it is this: The Ruling Elite is protected from the destructive consequences of its predatory behaviour. We see this reality across the entire political, social and economic landscape.

One chart that illustrates the widening divide between the Ruling Elite and the non-elites is this chart of wages as a share of the nation's GDP: 45 years of relentless decline, interrupted by gushing fountains of credit and asset bubbles that enriched the few while leaving the economic landscape of the many in ruins.

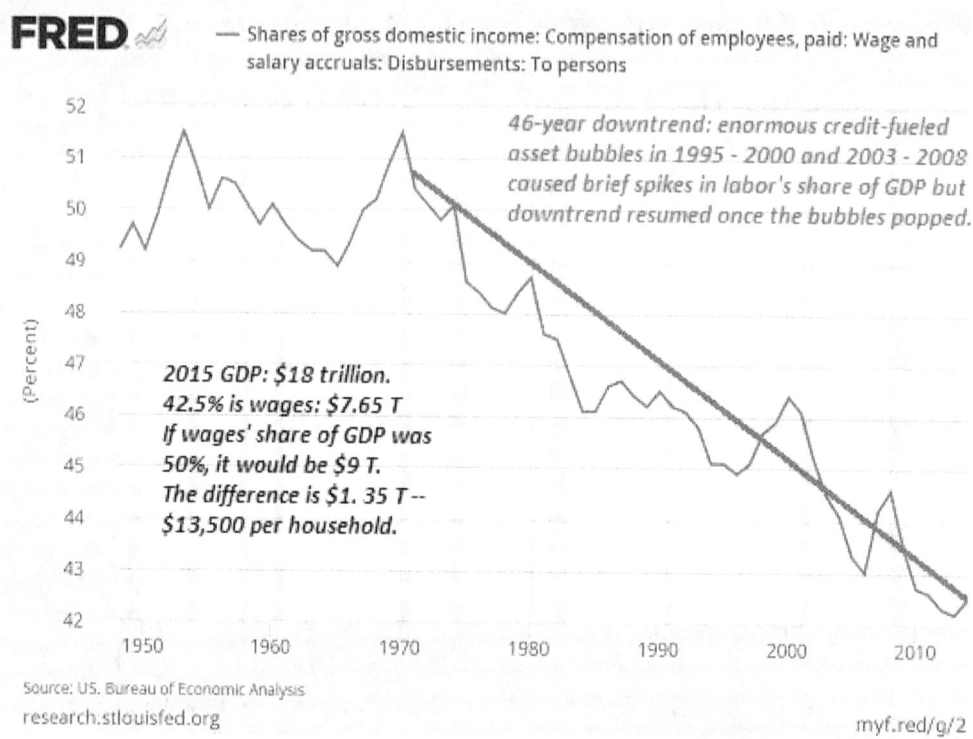

FRED — Shares of gross domestic income: Compensation of employees, paid: Wage and salary accruals: Disbursements: To persons

46-year downtrend: enormous credit-fueled asset bubbles in 1995 - 2000 and 2003 - 2008 caused brief spikes in labor's share of GDP but downtrend resumed once the bubbles popped.

2015 GDP: $18 trillion.
42.5% is wages: $7.65 T
If wages' share of GDP was
50%, it would be $9 T.
The difference is $1. 35 T --
$13,500 per household.

Source: U.S. Bureau of Economic Analysis
research.stlouisfed.org

myf.red/g/2

The elites once had an obligation to uphold the social contract as a responsibility that came with their vast privilege, power and wealth.

America's ruling elites have transformed themselves into an incestuous self-serving few unapologetically plundering the many. In their arrogance, their right to rule is unquestioningly based on their moral and intellectual superiority to "the little people" they loot with abandon.

Rather than feel a responsibility to the nation, American elites view the status quo as a free pass to self-aggrandizement. Much has changed in America in the past 46 years. Not only have wages and salaries declined as a share of "economic growth," but the wealth that has been generated has flowed to the top of the pyramid.

The economy is rapidly undergoing structural changes that tend to reward the top 5% class of technocrats and managers and the top .1% with millions in mobile capital, while leaving the bottom 95% in the dust.

The ever-widening wage gap

The chart below shows the growing change since 1973 to wages among me: top and middle of the earnings distribution.

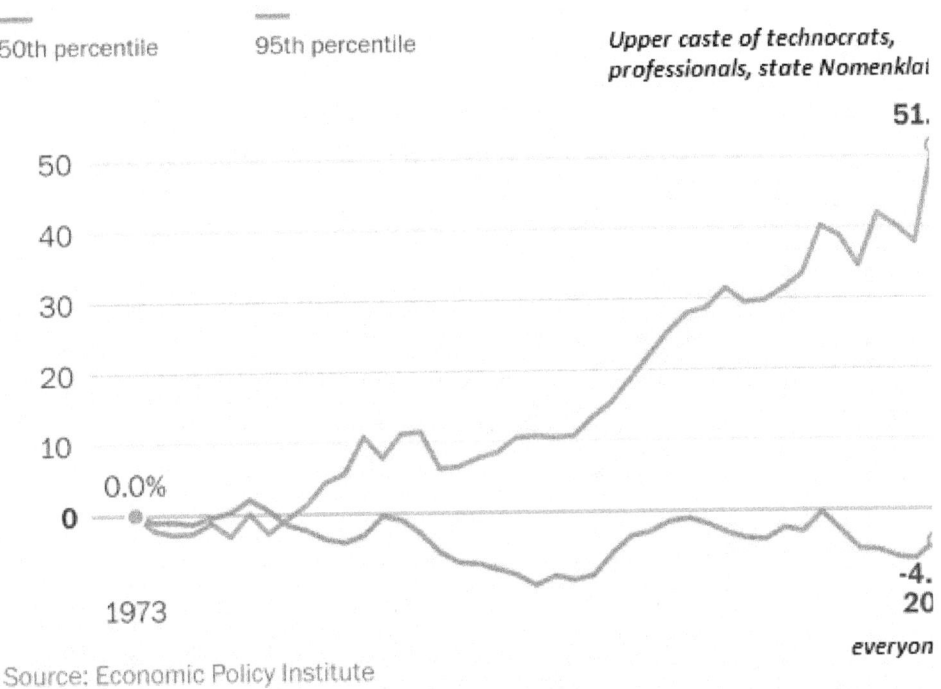

50th percentile   95th percentile   *Upper caste of technocrats, professionals, state Nomenklai*

Source: Economic Policy Institute

THE WASHINGTON POST

Truth Is The Enemy Of The State

The day before the 2016 US Presidential Election, most pollsters and statistical models had pegged Hillary Clinton's chances of winning at greater than 90%. For Wisconsin, Michigan, Pennsylvania, and New Hampshire; not a single source gave an edge to Republicans.

After 30 years of misrule and planting the seeds of economic and financial ruin throughout America, the Wall Street/Washington establishment and its mainstream media lapdogs have been repudiated like never before in modern history.

During the course of the past year, upwards of 70 million citizens; 59 million for Trump & 13 million for Bernie Sanders, voted for dramatic change. That is, for an end to pointless and failed wars and interventions abroad and a bubble-based economic policy at home.

The voters also said in no uncertain terms that they are fed-up with a "rigged" system that has one set of rules for establishment insiders and another for everyone else. That's what the Clinton Foundation pay-to-play scandals and the trove of Wikileaks DNC/Podesta hacks was all about.

Brexit-ed

The parallels between the U.K.'s shocking approval of the Brexit referendum in June and the U.S.' even more shocking election of Trump as president are stunning. Elites aggressively unified across ideological lines in opposition to both. Supporters of Brexit and Trump were relentlessly maligned by the dominant media narrative as primitive, racist, and irrational. The elites whose entitlement to prevail was crushed, devoted their energies to blaming everyone they could find except for themselves, while doubling down on their unbridled contempt for those who defied them, refusing to analyse the real causes of their loss.

The indisputable fact is that prevailing institutions of authority in the West, for decades, have relentlessly and with complete indifference stomped on the economic welfare of hundreds of millions of people. While elite circles gorged themselves on globalism, free trade, Wall Street casino gambling, and endless wars (wars that enriched the defense contractors and sent the poorest and most marginalized to bear all their burdens as soldiers), they completely ignored the victims, except when those victims rebelled against the established order.

The message was heard loud and clear. The institutions and elite factions that have spent years mocking, maligning, and pillaging large portions of the population, are now shocked that their dictates and decrees go ignored. But citizens are not going to follow and obey the exact people they most blame for their suffering. They're going to do exactly the opposite: purposely defy them and try to impose punishment in retaliation.

Their instruments for retaliation were Brexit and Trump.

For many years, the U.S. — like the U.K. and other Western nations — has embarked on a course that virtually guaranteed a collapse of elite authority and internal implosion. From the invasion of Iraq to the 2008 financial crisis, societal benefits have been directed almost exclusively to the very elite institutions most responsible for failure at the expense of everyone else.

It was only a matter of time before instability, backlash, and disruption resulted. Both Brexit and Trump unmistakably signal its arrival. The only question is whether those two cataclysmic events will be the peak of this process, or just the beginning. And that, in turn, will be determined by whether their crucial lessons are learned or ignored in favor of self-exonerating campaigns to blame everyone else.

Trump proved that creating enthusiasm among an electorate is way more important than spending $100's of millions of dollars on developing a "ground game."

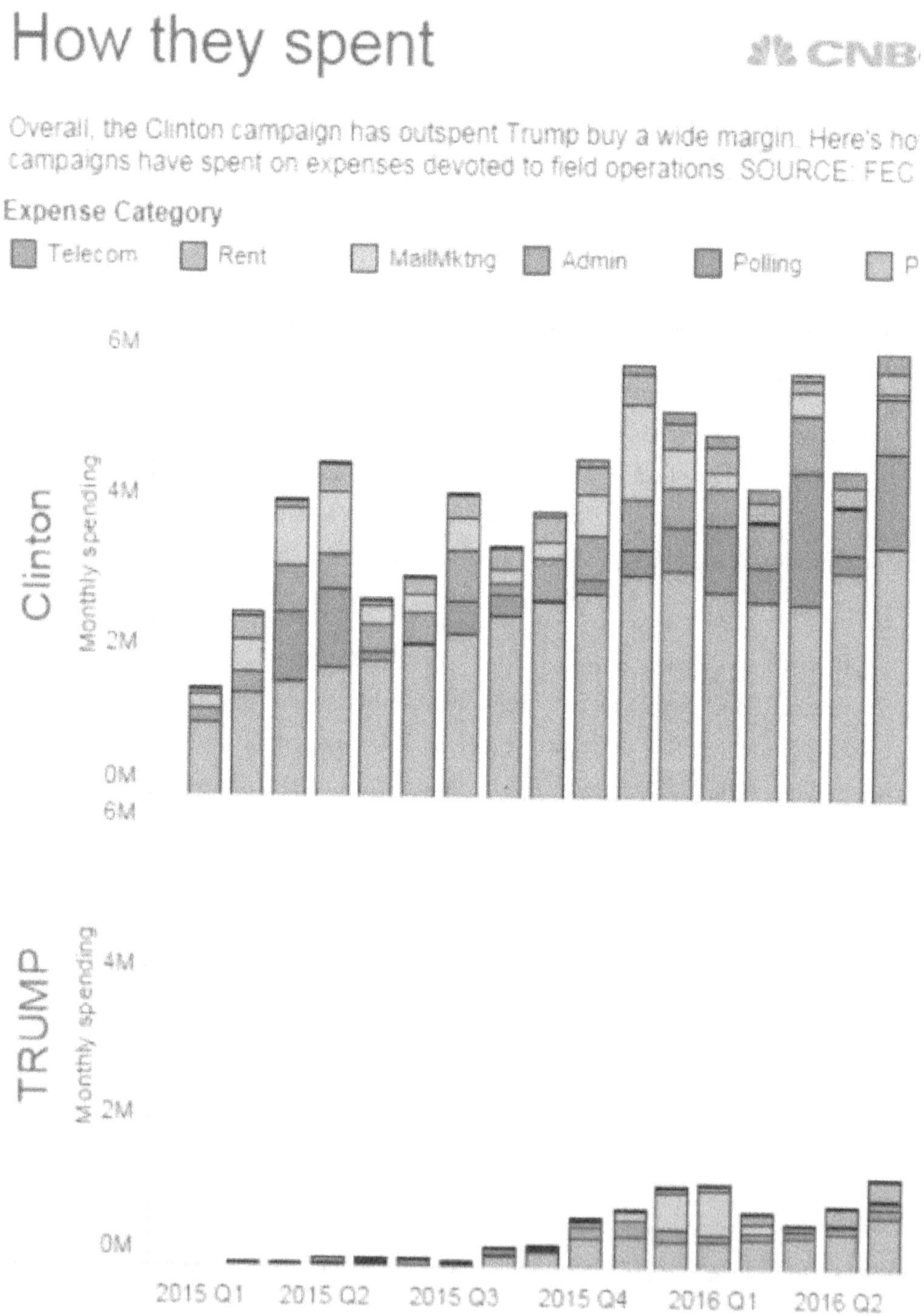
How they spent
CNB
Overall, the Clinton campaign has outspent Trump buy a wide margin. Here's ho
campaigns have spent on expenses devoted to field operations. SOURCE: FEC
Expense Category
Telecom
Rent
MailMktng
Admin
Polling
P
Clinton
Monthly spending
6M
4M
2M
0M
TRUMP
Monthly spending
6M
4M
2M
0M
2015 Q1
2015 Q2
2015 Q3
2015 Q4
2016 Q1
2016 Q2

Part II

Just like with Brexit, the so-called Wall Street experts scrambled to paint a picture of doom and gloom, warning traders, and markets, that the end of the world is imminent should Trump win, and that stocks could drop by 5%, 10% or more should Donald Trump get elected president.

Trump's victory increases the chance of higher fiscal spending but it will also reinforce the backlash against globalisation and associated forces of which migration policy and trade are obviously likely to be heavily scrutinised. So as the trend is already pointing to higher volatility.

First Brexit, now Trump. The political world is changing and the consequences are likely huge over the years ahead. Economists are likely to lower growth estimates due to "policy uncertainty". Trump's victory could temporarily derail stronger growth, higher rates narrative by raising expectations of
a) protectionism,
b) the Italian referendum following Brexit and US election as repudiation of elites.

Trump's criticism of Fed Chair Yellen is likely to unsettle global Treasury investors. On fiscal policy, he will likely push for tax cuts for individuals and businesses and a bipartisan deal to repatriate $2tn in foreign earnings at lower tax rates to fund federal infrastructure spending.

Uncertainty shock equals lower US GDP estimates; markets will price in EU fragmentation; Ultimate growth impact of Trump will depend on whether his protectionism or Keynesianism triumphs.

A Pyrrhic Victory?

Trump is walking into the Oval Office in January, it is only because the elites decided to put him there in advance, and for a reason. His win means the global economic collapse the system has been holding off on will finally come to pass under Trump's watch.

Even if Trump is a legitimate anti-establishment conservative, his entry into the Oval Office will seal the deal on the economic collapse, and will serve the globalists well. The international banks need only pull the plug on any remaining life support to the existing market system and allow it to fully implode, all while blaming Trump and his conservative supporters for the insanity.

He will be the perfect scapegoat for something the alternative media have known is coming for a long, long time. It's not much of a secret that the economy is being artificially propped up. The Fed's QE stimulus programs are no longer working. We know it can't remain this way forever.

Breakdown!

If we can all agree on one thing, it's that the government and disaster organizations alike grossly underestimate how dependent the majority of the population is on them during and after a disastrous event takes place. We need not look any further than the last major disasters that have occurred to find our answers: the Haitian earthquake that occurred in 2010, Hurricane Katrina in 2005, and even as recently as Hurricane Sandy.

When the needs of the population cannot be met in an allotted time frame, a phenomena occurs and the mindset shifts in people. They begin to act without thinking and respond to changes in their environment in an emotionally-based manner, thus leading to chaos, instability and a breakdown in our social paradigm.

When you take the time to understand how a breakdown behaves and how it progresses, only then can you truly prepare for it. Although disasters such as earthquakes and tornadoes can come on so quickly that timely warnings are not always given, for the most part, governments typically provide adequate time to get a population ready in advance. Local governments even go as far as to err on the side of caution and sternly warn the citizens to evacuate.

For one reason or another, there will be a select group that stays behind. Some of these citizens are prepared and ready for what may come and may feel the need to stay to defend what is rightfully theirs but the majority of the population will not be ready.

This is the point in this cycle where herds of people go to the grocery stores frantically grabbing supplies. Most grocery stores will not be able to meet the demand of the people's need for supplies, and many could go home empty handed. Study what happened in Venezuala, for example.

Bracing for the disaster, the prepared and unprepared will be hoping for the best outcome. What many do not realize is the hardest part of this event is soon to be upon them. Within days, the descent into the breakdown will begin.

At this point, the unprepared survivors will be expecting organizations and local government to step in to meet their immediate needs at any moment. The reality of the situation becomes more bleak when they realize that due to downed power lines or debris blocking roadways and access points, emergency organizations, emergency response and distribution trucks supplying food, water, fuel and other pertinent resources will be unable to get to the area. Once the realization hits that resources are scarce and the government leaders are incapable of helping them in a timely fashion, desperate citizens will take action into their own hands.

The breakdown begins.

Part III

The first industrial revolution was all about Western Europe, with England as the predominant actor. The foundation for the British Empire was laid and the unipolar world that followed was relatively stable with Britain as the undisputed hegemon.

The second industrial revolution quickly spread to Germany and the US. Not long after, the British economy lost its preeminent place a manufacturer of the world. Britain understood that the unipolar world its empire represented would be lost unless the newfound players could be contained. Germany in particular was keen on an empire and started its exploits in Africa in the 1880s to the detriment of an expanding British empire.

The straw that probably broke British patience was the German-funded railway to the Middle East. When completed the Brits, as the unquestionable global naval power, would lose control over German oil supplies. The Germans would also gain access to the port of Basra, avoiding the Suez Canal for access to the eastern part of the German colonial empire. German demand for more "Lebensraum" obviously did not go down well with Westminster. The tragic end result was the industrial killing of Europeans on a scale never witnessed before.

By taking on Germany, Britain tried to bite off more than it could chew. Britain ended up bankrupt and the US emerged as the largest creditor nation on the planet. While it took some time to make the transition, by the end of World War II the US was the undisputable super power. However, this was merely a change of headquarter as the Imperial City of the British empire moved from London to New York. Culturally the two nations were and still are close; and to this day the special relationship between Britain and the US is cultivated more than any.

Still, the key takeaway from the period stretching between 1880s to 1914 (or 1945) is one where the world hegemon experience relative decline as its manufacturing base is outcompeted by technologically advancing competitors amid a deteriorating balance of payment. The end result was a world in turmoil with legacy structures, be it political and economic, changing beyond recognition.

While history never repeats itself, it certainly rhymes and today's situation is in many respects quite similar to the pre-WWI period. Once again, we have a global hegemon going deeper and deeper into debt. A balance of payment problem, funded by the "exorbitant privilege" of issuing the global reserve currency, has transformed the US from the world's largest creditor nations to the largest debtor.

Emerging economies thus feel confident when threatening the US dominance by increasingly making their presence felt in what used to be US (or US satellite states) exclusive territory. China in particular claim surrounding waters as its playground and a more assertive Russia has started to fight back against NATO mission creep.

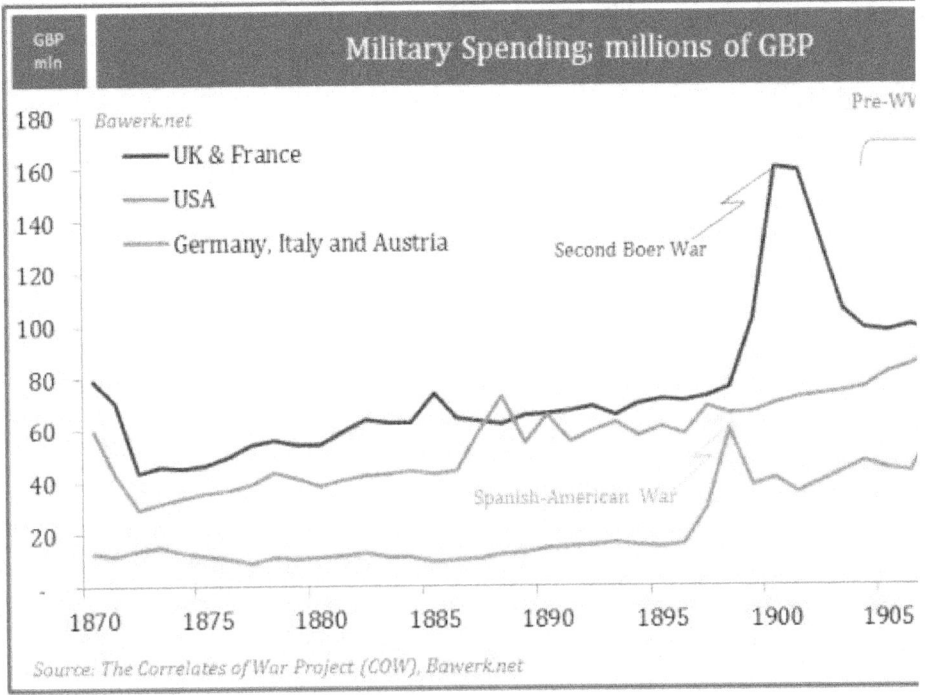

Military Spending; millions of GBP

GBP min

Source: The Correlates of War Project (COW), Bawerk.net

Just as in the pre-WWI era, military spending by potential adversaries is catching up with the hegemon. Proxy wars are increasingly being fought as the world move toward a multipolar world order. As history has shown, the transition from a unipolar to a multipolar world can be taxing and unfortunately bloody. It is also worth noting that the Beijing consensus is materially different from the London/Washington worldview. While moving the Imperial City from London to Washington was not all bad for Europe, another move to Beijing could be far more disruptive.

The world economy and by extension, political constellations are due for changes unprecedented in later modern history. Finally, it will be more than interesting to see either a Trump presidency tread what will undoubtedly be very treacherous waters.

Part IV

Remember the story your parents and teachers told you, about how Socialism tries to increase the wealth of the Lower Orders by increasing their share of "the pie", but fails because
1) there are too many Workers for them to get more than the tiniest piece each and
2) the effects of Socialism cause The Pie itself to shrink?

While Capitalism causes The Pie to constantly get bigger and bigger, and thus while the Little People still get much smaller shares than The Great, their wealth grows because the Pie itself grows from the salutary effects of incentives and Hard Work? That one? It's a lie.

The American Pie grew stupendously during the period from 1945 to 1980 because America was
1) the only large industrial economy left functioning after WWII; and
2) adopted numerous government policies that were downright Socialist to make sure that wealth didn't migrate primarily to the already wealthy from 1945-1970.
Both situations were reversed after 1980, and The Pie stopped growing.

Growth of the Pie had nothing to do with the grand benefits of The Capitalist System. That was pure hogwash from the day that Adam Smith created it out of whole cloth as part of a marketing campaign for his industrialist buddies.

The American Pie grew because of a uniquely fortuitous combination of resources -- an entire continent newly-stolen from its former inhabitants combined with the collapse of Europe into self-demolishing internecine strife after Europe had laid waste to the ancient civilizations of Asia.

Now that Asia is recovering, Europe is peaceful, and America has exploited all of it's easily accessed resources, the system as a whole is rebalancing. And the flat, irremediable fact is, INFINITE GROWTH IS IMPOSSIBLE IN A FINITE WORLD.

All of the growth curves are flattening back to steady-state, because in the long run, steady-state is the best you can hope for. You CAN'T HAVE GROWTH FOREVER. Sorry. It just doesn't work that way.

Pretty much everything your parents and teachers told you was a lie. They didn't mean it that way. But everything THEY were told and believed was pure bunkum, too, and they passed it down to you.

"After four years of warfare that tore the world apart like never before, a peace was finally reached. But it was a peace which one man in particular vociferously condemned — and that man was John Maynard Keynes. Keynes was highly critical of the deal struck at Versailles, which he felt sure would lead to further conflict in Europe — describing the agreement as a "Carthaginian peace" — and with the passing of a surprisingly short period of time, he would be proven correct."

After WWI, a particularly noxious set of treaties and economic reparations agreements were put in place that all but guaranteed a future WWII. Mr. Keynes sniffed that out and, sadly, was proven correct.

The lesson from this is that, at certain times, it's really not that hard to predict "what" is going to happen next after disastrously short-sighted and self-interested policies are enacted. Predicting the "when", with precision, is much trickier. But obvious misguided economic policies are destined to have a limited period of apparent (but false) prosperity, after which they end with a nasty collapse.

We have entered just such a time.

The economic "peace" we've seemingly enjoyed over the past number of decades turned out to be no peace at all. It was the same sort of peace that existed between the Treaty of Versailles and the outbreak of WWII -- a crippling arrangement that overwhelmingly favored one side over the other. Germany eventually had no choice but to rebel.

Similarly, by failing to protect anyone but their cloistered and wealthy friends, the elites of both current US political parties has laid the fuel for the fire that now burns.

When you add up both the debts and the liabilities of the US, those are more than 1,000% of current GDP.

No country has ever dug out from under such a load. None have even come close. The "prediction," which is so simple it's not really a prediction at all, that flows from the above chart is this: Somebody is going to have to eat the losses. Massive, fabulously enormous losses. Trillions of losses in current dollars. Even if the elites don't try to force all of those losses on the 'little people', the pain is still going to be so extraordinary that serious political and social crises will erupt.

THERE ARE TOO MANY PROMISES THAT CAN'T BE KEPT

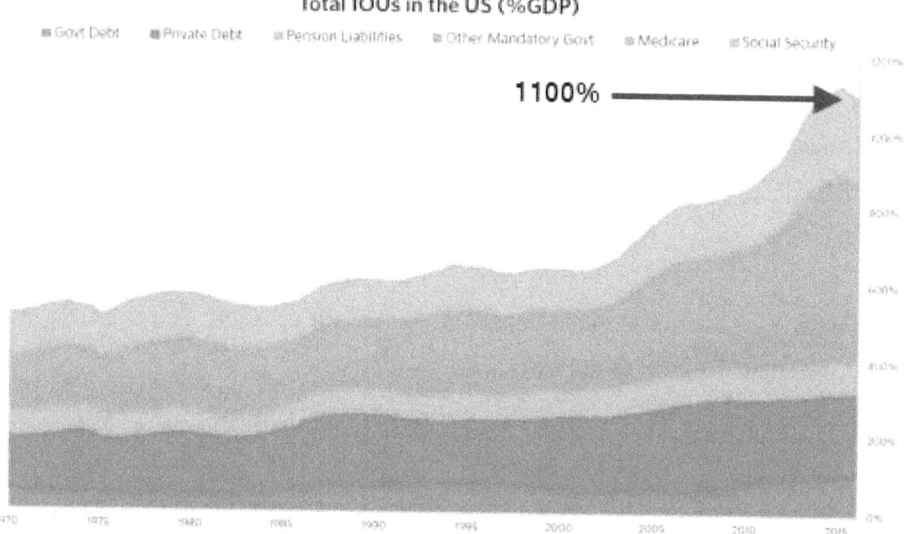

Total IOUs in the US (%GDP)

Note: Medicare, Social Security and other government programs represents the present value of estimates of future outlays from the Congressional Budget Office.

BRIDGEWATER

You can already see that larger future predicament playing out painfully around us. One example is how pensions are cutting back benefits, lowering expectations, demanding higher funding payments by taxpayers, and otherwise displaying signs of distress. So our recent decades of economic peace must end, given the thousand percent indebtedness predicament.

We got into that thousand percent predicament the exact same way the DNC lost to Trump: by failing to address things that plainly needed to be dealt with. We proved to ourselves, yet again, that pretending something uncomfortable doesn't exist doesn't make it go away.

If GDP had been growing at the same pace, the ratio value wouldn't have budged. It would have remained at 700%. But it grew to 1,100%, which means the debts and obligations were growing much faster than GDP.

So for the past 15 years the "grow out of it" mantra -- which has been echoed ad nauseum -- has been a complete train wreck of a failure. How many more years before we can all just admit the obvious?

Just as both the RNC and DNC opted to ignore the extreme damage their policies had been inflicting on the upper, middle and lower classes, sparing only the very tippy-top elites (but hand-feeding those elites peeled grapes it should be noted, because their lot improved wildly over the past decades), everybody in power has been steadfastly ignoring our massive debt and liability problems, too. Those are going to shape the future, and that future is going to be plenty painful. The longer we wait, the more painful it will be.

The political upheaval of Donald Trump is best understood through the lens of economic erosion suffered by the vast majority of people. It will take an enormous amount of effort simply to stem the tide of economic erosion that now besets the land. And that's just as true for the US as it is for Japan, Europe and the UK. The same forces are at play in all of these centers.

It will take another massive bowlful of effort to begin to address the debts and liabilities issues. And yet another cauldron of effort to revamp our energy infrastructure in parallel with all the other challenges. Put it all together and you can begin to understand why, if we're going to deplore something from the recent election, it should be the running of an intentionally divisive set of campaigns that have driven as large a wedge between people in the US as has existed in a very long time.

Part V

When the economic storm hits, it will be a Catagory 6 Shit Storm that will have corn and nuts in it.

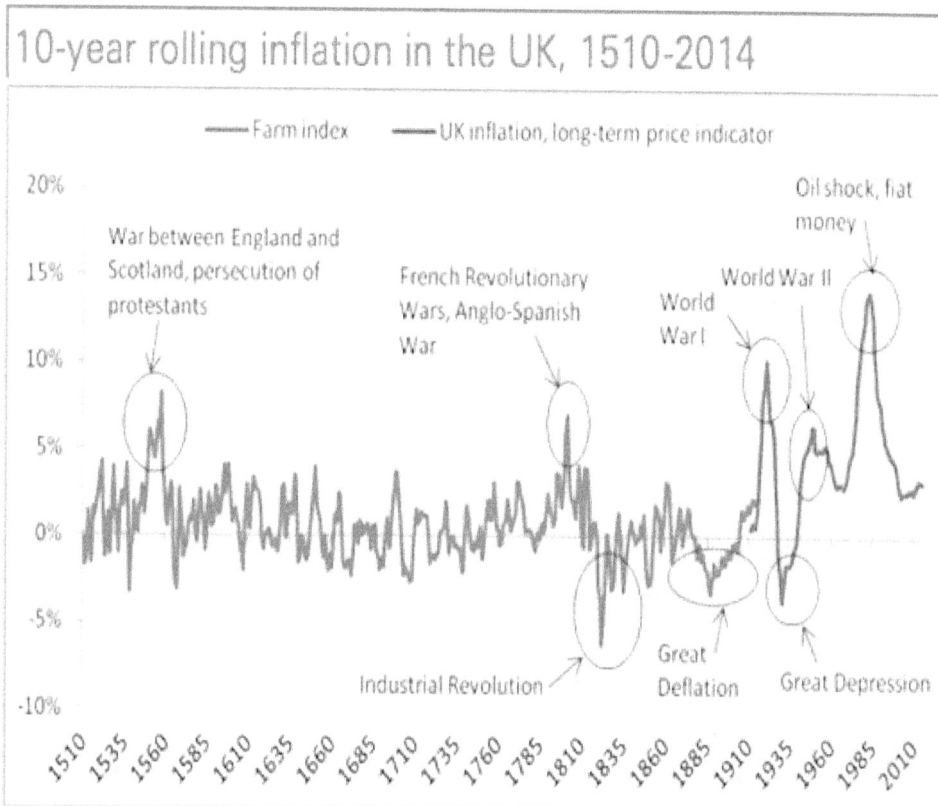

10-year rolling inflation in the UK, 1510-2014

For the first four hundred years depicted here, money was gold and silver — the quantity of which rose at roughly the same rate as the human population. Prices during that time fluctuated, but only modestly by today's standards, and they always returned to more-or-less the same level. In other words, money held its value for not just years but centuries. It was a fixed aspect of the financial environment and was therefore not a tool of economic policy. Governments and individuals had to adapt to unchanging money rather than forcing money to adapt to political circumstances.

A phase change occurs in the 20th century when the US created the Federal Reserve and World Wars I and II placed survival above monetary stability for most of Europe and Asia. Violent swings in the value of money became the norm, and with the subsequent worldwide adoption of fiat currencies — which governments can create at will — volatility has soared.

Clearly, something bad has happened — and just as clearly something really bad is coming.

An Epic Fiat Currency Avalanche

What is it that makes Keynesians so insanely self destructive? Is it their mindless blind faith in the power of government? Their unfortunate ignorance of the mechanics of monetary stimulus? Their pompous self-righteousness derived from years of intellectual idiocy? Needless to say, many of them truly believe that the strategy of fiat injection is viable, even though years of application have proven absolutely fruitless. Anyone with any sense would begin to question what kind of madness it takes to pursue or champion the mindset of the private Federal Reserve bank…

Quantitative easing has shown itself to be impotent in the improvement of America's economic situation. Despite four years of free reign in central banking, employment remains dismal in the U.S., the housing market continues its freefall, and, our national debt swirls like a vortex at the heart of the Bermuda Triangle. Despite this abject failure of Keynesian theory, the Federal Reserve is attempting once again to convince you, the happy-go-lucky American citizen, that somehow, this time around, everything will be "different".

Open ended inflation is exactly what destroyed Weimar Germany, and more recently Zimbabwe. The central banks and their lackeys will claim there is no comparison. When a nation expands debt spending instead of cutting it, and then monetizes that debt through fiat printing in order to allow even more debt to accumulate, that nation is not going to survive. That nation will eventually hyperinflate, then default, then collapse, either turning into something entirely alien, or fading from history altogether. This is what we have to look forward to in light of QE3, the final and infinite stimulus adventure. Something has to give, and it has to give soon.

"The collapse of the people's confidence in the created money, which was forced upon them by legal tender laws, will have a bad effect upon the government. It would be to the advantage of those really in charge to avert a total loss of confidence in their created money, to declare bankruptcy, initiate a deflation, returning so much wealth on the dollar and issuing a new redeemable one, if only to continue their power over us. It is inevitable, we will see a tremendous depression and a return to gold and silver as wealth mediums of exchange – it has always gone that way." – Money: The Greatest Hoax on Earth, Merrill Jenkins, 1971, Pg 150.

Technology will make governments obsolete. Name a reason for big government besides security. Mutually assured destruction keeps moving lower on the economic chain. Soon anyone with a bio-workstation will be able to fashion viruses to kill whatever they want. Technology will make energy production local. After energy will come water. After water will come food. All local. The internet makes commuter education irrelevant. Decision making will become regional again. Big governments will fail. Already happening. USSR gone. EU going away. USA and China, probably will unravel in the next 20 years. Canada the same. Back to government by provinces and states. The way it should be.

"Throughout its nearly 100-year history, the Federal Reserve has presided over the near-complete destruction of the United States dollar. Since 1913 the dollar has lost over 95 percent of its purchasing power, aided and abetted by the Federal Reserve's loose monetary policy." --- Ron Paul.

History records that in 1913 President Woodrow Wilson approved the Federal Reserve Act but later reflected that his actions "unwittingly ruined my country."

Wilson said that since the U.S. system of credit is concentrated in the hands of a few, "we have become ... one of the most completely controlled and dominated governments in the civilized world."

When the Roman Empire collapsed during the reign of Gallienus (253-268 AD), for the next two waves of the Economic Confidence Model (17.2 years) Rome remained in chaos. Then a general fought his way to power – Diocletian (284-305AD). During this period, inflation soared. Money really became in kind and the purchasing power of the debased coinage collapsed with the lack of confidence in government. This became akin to the crisis in Germany during the 1920s. People simply did not really accept the debased Roman coinage.

'Monetary Heroin'

"It's not going to be a painless situation when we give up these government narcotics -- monetary heroin -- but it's going to have to happen, because the more we take this drug, the more damage is being done to the economy and the risk is, of course, that eventually we overdose on it, which is the destruction of the currency and a runaway inflation," --- Peter Schiff.

We refer to the dollar as a "reserve currency" when referring to its use by other countries when settling their international trade accounts. For example, if Canada buys goods from China, China may prefer to be paid in US dollars rather than Canadian dollars. The US dollar is the more "marketable" money internationally, meaning that most countries will accept it in payment, so China can use its dollars to buy goods from other countries, not solely the US. Such might not be the case with the Canadian dollar, and China would have to hold its Canadian dollars until it found something to buy from Canada. Multiply this scenario by all the countries of the world who print their own money and one can see that without a currency accepted widely in the world, international trade would slow down and become more expensive. Its effect would be similar to that of erecting trade barriers, such as the infamous Smoot-Hawley Tariff of 1930 that contributed to the Great Depression. There are many who draw a link between the collapse of international trade and war. The great French economist Frederic Bastiat said that "when goods do not cross borders, soldiers will." No nation can achieve a decent standard of living with a completely autarkic economy, meaning completely self-sufficient in all things. If it cannot trade for the goods that it needs, it feels forced to invade its neighbors to steal them. Thus, a near universally accepted currency is as vital to world peace as it is to world prosperity.

However, the foundation from which the term "reserve currency" originated no longer exists.

Originally the term "reserve" referred to the promise that the currency was backed by and could be redeemed for a commodity, usually gold, at a promised exchange ratio. The first truly global reserve currency was the British Pound Sterling. Because the Pound was "good as gold", many countries found it more convenient to hold Pounds rather than gold itself during the age of the gold standard. The world's great trading nations settled their trade in gold, but they might accept Pounds rather than gold, with the confidence that the Bank of England would hand over the gold at a fixed exchange rate upon presentment. Toward the end of World War II the US dollar was given this status by treaty following the Bretton Woods Agreement.

The US accumulated the lion's share of the world's gold as the "arsenal of democracy" for the allies even before we entered the war. The International Monetary Fund (IMF) was formed with the express purpose of monitoring the Federal Reserve's commitment to Bretton Woods by ensuring that the Fed did not inflate the dollar and stood ready to exchange dollars for gold at $35 per ounce. Countries had confidence that their dollars held for trading purposes were as "good as gold", as had been the British Pound at one time.

However, the Fed did not maintain its commitment to the Bretton Woods Agreement and the IMF did not attempt to force it to hold enough gold to honor all its outstanding currency in gold at $35 per ounce. During the 1960's the US funded the War in Vietnam and President Lyndon Johnson's War on Poverty with printed money. The volume of outstanding dollars exceeded the US's store of gold at $35 per ounce.

The Fed was called to account in the late 1960s first by the Bank of France and then by others. Central banks around the world, who had been content to hold dollars instead of gold, grew concerned that the US had sufficient gold reserves to honor its redemption promise. During the 1960's the run on the Fed, led by France, caused the US's gold stock to shrink dramatically from over 20,000 tons in 1958 to just over 8,000 tons in 1970.

At the accelerating rate that these redemptions were occurring, the US had no choice but to revalue the dollar at some higher exchange rate or abrogate its responsibilities to honor dollars for gold entirely. To its everlasting shame, the US chose the latter and "went off the gold standard" in September 1971. (I have calculated that in 1971 the US would have needed to devalue the dollar from $35 per ounce to $400 per ounce in order to have sufficient gold stock to redeem all its currency for gold.) Nevertheless, the dollar was still held by the great trading nations, because it still performed the useful function of settling international trading accounts. There was no other currency that could match the dollar, despite the fact that it was "delinked" from gold.

There are two characteristics of a currency that make it useful in international trade: one, it is issued by a large trading nation itself, and, two, the currency holds its value over time. These two factors create a demand for holding a currency in reserve. Although the dollar was being inflated by the Fed, thusly losing its value vis a vis other commodities over time, there was no real competition.

The German Deutsche Mark held its value better, but the German economy and its trade was a fraction that of the US, meaning that holders of marks would find less to buy in Germany than holders of dollars would find in the US. So demand for the mark was lower than demand for the dollar. Of course, psychological factors entered the demand for dollars, too, since the US was the military protector of all the Western nations against the communist countries.

Today we are seeing the beginnings of a change.

Part VI

The "perfect storm" of concurrent failures in US policy across foreign, monetary, economic, and fiscal fronts!

If you look at the entire radar screen of things developing both domestically and internationally, we are plunging deep into a perfect storm of policy failure. The American Imperium is collapsing. There is blowback everywhere. The wreckage of prior policy mistakes of our intervention with foreign policy is coming home to roost, and the Ukraine is one area at ground zero for that.

But second, monetary central planning is now coming to a dead-end. It is inflating the third financial bubble of the century and the Fed is now clueless as to how it will manage to unwind the massive balance sheet expansion it has been undertaken.

And third, the fiscal doomsday machine continues to crank on. Washington is ignoring the fact that we are six years into a business cycle expansion and we are still running massive deficits and there is no cushion for the next upset that comes to the economy.

Now, why is all of this important? Because I think the foreign policy failures -- the collapse of the American Imperium as I call it -- is at the center of this, and it will push all of these things in the wrong direction.

We are now becoming much more aggressive in our foreign policy than ever before. We can't afford it by any means. And the potential for this to create black swans to roil or dislocate these very fragile markets that have been created by this massive central bank balance sheet expansion -- it all makes what is happening in the Ukraine, or in the Middle East in Gaza, or in the collapse of Iraq, even more dangerous in terms of what it could trigger. So we are in a real pickle here and it is compounding by the day.

At risk here is America's capability to remain the world's dominant superpower.

It's just the warfare state machinery has gotten itself activated into motion and it is drastically simplifying the real facts that we face and creating a narrative that is really preposterous in terms of what our national security, the safety and security of the American people, really requires in this circumstance.

The Dragon Tail

For the first time in history, China docked a Navy Destroyer in a Southern Iranian port of Bandar-Abbas - right across the Straits of Hormuz.

Middle East Energy Production & Chokepoir

Percent of global liquid fuel production, 2012*

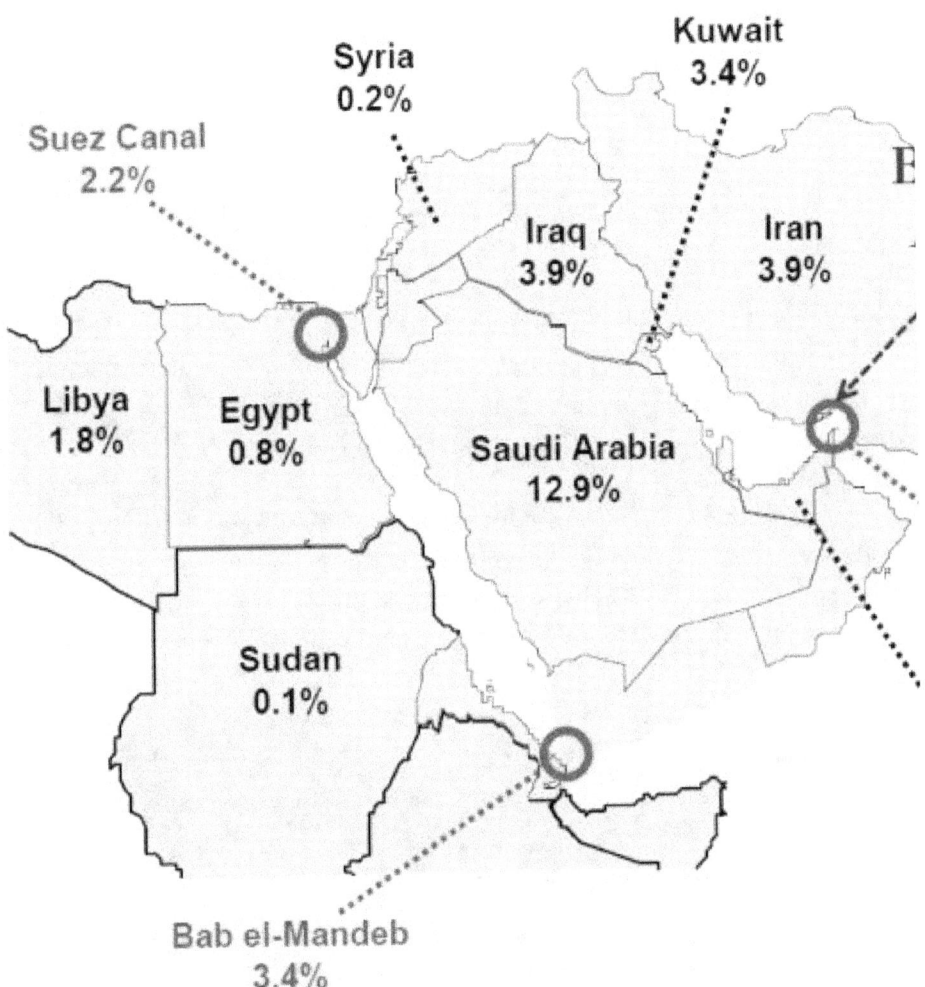

Syria 0.2%

Kuwait 3.4%

Suez Canal 2.2%

Iraq 3.9%

Iran 3.9%

Libya 1.8%

Egypt 0.8%

Saudi Arabia 12.9%

Sudan 0.1%

Bab el-Mandeb 3.4%

Major Producers				Major Consumers			
Percent of global total, 2012				Percent of global total, 2012			
Saudi Arabia	13%	China	5%	United States	21%	India	
United States	12%	Canada	4%	China	11%	Russia	
Russia	12%	Iran	4%	Japan	5%	Saudi	

The move is seen as part of off efforts by Iran to strike a balance among foreign navies present in the area near the strategic Strait of Hormuz, the passageway at the mouth of the Persian Gulf through which a fifth of the world's oil is shipped.

U.S. Navy's 5th Fleet is based in nearby Bahrain, on the southern coast of the Gulf.

Why would the central bank of Nigeria decide to sell dollars and buy Yuan?

At first glance it might not seem the most interesting or pressing question for you to consider. But I think it is one of those little loose threads that if pulled upon carefully begins to unravel the hints and traces of a much larger story. But please be warned this is speculative.

Two days ago the Nigerian Central Bank announced it was going to increase the share of its foreign currency reserves held in Yuan from 2% at present, to up to 7%. To do this it was going to sell US Dollars. While it is small in raw financial terms I think it is significant in geopolitical terms.

Nigeria is Africa's second largest oil and gas exporter. It holds as many dollars as it does because oil is sold in dollars. Nigeria gets paid in dollars which it then needs to recycle. This is the famous petrodollar in action.

Islamist Jihad, the New Nazism?

Even before any major world powers were willing to go public (so to speak) with their involvement in Syria's five-year, bloody civil war, it was difficult to keep track of the myriad rebel factions, militant groups, and jihadists battling the Assad regime for control of the country.

In a testament to just how confusing (not to mention terrifying) the situation had become by the time Iran began to mull asking the Russians for help, 18,000 civilians ended up trapped in the Yarmouk refugee camp near Damascus where al-Nusra, ISIS, Hamas, the FSA, and the Assad regime were all fighting each other simultaneously in what UN Secretary General Ban ki-Moon called "the worst circle of hell."

At that juncture, the conflict was still largely a true proxy war. That is, sure there were probably some US Spec Ops running around with the Kurds and perhaps with the FSA and there were almost undoubtedly a handful of Iranian commanders shuttling back and forth between Damascus and Tehran while coordinating with Hezbollah, but the war didn't look anything like it does now in terms of overt military action by multiple world powers.

After Quds commander Qassem Soleimani visited the frontlines in Latakia in June, the general vowed to "surprise the world," with Iran's next move. Weeks later Soleimani was in Moscow plotting a Russian intervention with The Kremlin. By the end of September, Russia had built an air base at Latakia and on September 30, a three star general strolled into the US Embassy in Baghdad and informed the Americans that Russian airstrikes in Syria "began in 1 hour."

Now that the tense standoff between the US and Moscow looks set to usher in a new phase in the conflict characterized by world powers engaging one another directly, we thought it an opportune time to take inventory of who is who and what is what in Syria which just might be remembered as the theatre for the start of a Third World War.

A few dynamics unreported in detail in the mainstream media:

Russian fighter jets (now armed with air-to-air missiles) over Syria

- Russian missile cruisers off the Syrian coast protecting Russian assets on the ground and occasionally enforcing a no fly zone over the Mediterranean
- US, French fighter jets over Syria and Iraq
- The US Aircraft Carrier USS Harry Truman is set to arrive by the Syrian coast in a few weeks

- The French aircraft carrier Charles de Gaulle is parked off the Syrian coast
- UK fighter jets deployed over Syria within days
- German jets deployed over Syria within days
- German frigate to protect the French aircraft carrier
- German troops to be deployed
- US "special" troops officially deployed to Iraq, unofficially operating in Syria
- Russian "special" troops unofficially on the ground in Syria

The share of those who see the probability of World War III in the near future as high or very high is now at 48% and those who appraise it as low or very low comprise 42% of Russian society, according to the privately-owned public opinion research center Levada. The remaining 10% of respondents said they couldn't give a simple answer to the question.

It took 3 million soldiers, 3,000 tanks, 7,000 artillery pieces, and 2,500 aircraft…

"Operation Barbarossa" was the codename for Nazi Germany's invasion of the Soviet Union in 1941.

It was the largest military operation in human history. The Nazis had already conquered most of Europe. Hitler had grown overconfident from his recent military victories. Now he was hunting for big game… Stalin's USSR.

Throughout history, many European invaders, including Napoleon, suffered monumental defeats when they took on Russia. Despite this, Hitler thought he could succeed where they had failed. The idea was to inflict a total defeat on the Soviets in a matter of months, before the notoriously brutal Russian winter began.

At first, it looked like the Germans might succeed. The Soviets were taken by surprise and were disorganized. But those initial victories wouldn't be enough. Thanks to stubborn resistance and a seemingly inexhaustible supply of Soviet troops, Operation Barbarossa stalled.

The Germans didn't make it to Moscow before winter. The ruthless cold weather would prove to be a far more effective weapon than anything in the Soviet arsenal. Hitler's hopes of quickly taking out the USSR perished in the brutal cold. It ultimately turned the tide of the war against Germany.

But the Soviet victory cost millions of lives. By the end of the war, the Soviets had lost over 20 million people. Some estimate they lost many millions more. By comparison, the U.S. lost around 400,000 people.

So, it shouldn't be surprising that the Russians get a little prickly when a foreign military starts marching toward their borders. And recently… for the first time since Operation Barbarossa, German tanks are once again advancing on Russia's border.

You probably haven't heard this extraordinary piece of news. That's because the mass media has basically ignored and obscured it.

Operation Anaconda 2016.

It's the largest war game in Eastern Europe since the end of the Cold War. It's essentially a rehearsal to secure a quick NATO victory in the event of war with Russia. It was launched from Warsaw, Poland, recently and involves 31,000 NATO troops.

Operation Anaconda 2016 is one of the most important stories you're not hearing about. It shows how perilously close the world is to another global war.

U.S. politicians like to use Putin as a piñata to show how tough they are.

Hillary Clinton has declared Putin to be the new Hitler. This is the kind of thinking that fueled Operation Anaconda 2016.

Now, we're not referees charged with deciding which political players are good guys and which are bad guys. However, the portrait of Putin as a Hitler or a crazy man leading his country toward disaster—the picture you get from the mainstream media and from many politicians—is suitable only for propaganda posters.

Albert Einstein once said, "I know not with what weapons World War 3 will be fought, but World War 4 will be fought with sticks and stones."

Part VII

"History offers even more sobering warnings: Armed confrontation usually occurs around the climax of Crisis. If there is confrontation, it is likely to lead to war. This could be any kind of war – class war, sectional war, war against global anarchists or terrorists, or superpower war. If there is war, it is likely to culminate in total war, fought until the losing side has been rendered nil – its will broken, territory taken, and leaders captured." – The Fourth Turning – Strauss & Howe -1997.

It becomes painfully obvious this Fourth Turning is marching toward bloodshed, confrontation, and civil war. The linear fixated establishment, who fancy themselves intellectually superior to the irredeemable, are too blinded by their sociopathic, increasingly audacious subversion of the Constitution, to grasp the level of rage and disillusionment of a white working class that has been screwed over for decades.

As the Wall Street shysters frantically accelerate their embezzlement of what remains of middle class wealth, with the Fed and the corporate media propagandists as their wingmen, the country devolves into a corporate fascist state. The disposition of the nation grows dark like the sky before an approaching deadly blizzard. As passions boil over and violence portends, this Fourth Turning hastens towards a bloody decade ahead with an uncertain climax.

If you think this is just hyperbole, you either haven't studied history or your cognitive dissonance and normalcy bias prevent you from seeing the unavoidable societal altering clashes, which occur like clockwork on an eighty year cycle, when the portents are right in front of your eyes. Historian Arnold Toynbee's great war cycle that arise every 80 years or so, aligns perfectly with the Fourth Turning generational theory. Great wars occur when the generation that doesn't remember the last catastrophic war ascends to leadership of the country.

We are eight years into a Crisis period which won't end until the mid-2020s. As this bitterly vicious presidential campaign accelerates towards a finale which will leave the country divided and irate, the hostile opposing forces will be seeking revenge, retribution, and retaliation no matter the outcome. There is no doubt the degeneracy is well under way.

"The next Fourth Turning is due to begin shortly after the new millennium, midway through the Oh-Oh decade. Around the year 2005, a sudden spark will catalyze a Crisis mood. Remnants of the old social order will disintegrate. Political and economic trust will implode. Real hardship will beset the land, with severe distress that could involve questions of class, race, nation and empire. The very survival of the nation will feel at stake. Sometime before the year 2025, America will pass through a great gate in history, commensurate with the American Revolution, Civil War, and twin emergencies of the Great Depression and World War II." – Strauss & Howe – The Fourth Turning

Neil Howe was particularly worried about the Federal Reserve zero interest rate policy and how it was ruining our economic system, creating disincentives to saving and encouraging warped, debt driven speculation. And that was in 2011. The Fed keeping interest rates near zero on behalf of a corrupt establishment for the last eight years has been the primary factor in creating the anger, disillusionment and revolutionary spirit driving the regeneracy.

No critical thinking human being can deny this tumultuous presidential election and its equally turbulent primaries have been fueled by the dreadful self-serving response of the establishment to the 2008 Wall Street created financial collapse; the geopolitical anarchy created by U.S. interventionism in the Middle East; the civic decay created by a failing government educational system; rampant debt financed materialism enabled and encouraged by the financial/media complex; and racial division facilitated by the president and his social justice warrior brethren.

The rescue of Wall Street and destruction of Main Street by the Fed, Wall Street and the captured politicians of both parties in Washington D.C. has created the angry, acrimonious, throw the bums out mood boiling over in flyover America. The widening Grand Canyon gap in wealth between the haves and the have nots, produced by solutions from sociopaths in suits has reached the pitchfork and torch level.

The linear thinking ruling class has been in denial since this Crisis catalyzed in September 2008. Their looting, pillaging and ransacking campaign, designed to enrich and empower a small cadre of shadowy, powerful, wealthy men, had been successful for decades. When you control the currency and interest rates; rig the financial markets; buy the politicians; write the laws and regulations; own the corporate propaganda machines known as the mainstream media; operate a high tech surveillance state; create a dumbed down populace through government school indoctrination; and distract the masses with iGadgets, reality TV, hero worship, professional sports, social media, irrelevant cultural issues, and literally thousands of other modern day bread and circuses; you become arrogant and careless.

These sociopaths are so consumed with their ravenous fleecing of the middle class, waging wars for profit, and shredding the Constitution, they failed to recognize 2008 for the seismic earth shattering event that will change everything. The mood of the country shifted like tectonic plates beneath the nation. The mood continues to grow dimmer, as the peasants grow poorer and the modern day aristocracy (Wall Street bankers, corporate executives, corrupt politicians, shadowy billionaires) accumulate obscene ill-gotten wealth through their complete capture of the system. This perverted, degenerative, criminal degradation of our society is powerfully summed up by Jesse from Jesse's Café Americain:

"Not all sociopaths wield knives and knotted cords. Some wear suits, and are exceptionally intelligent and articulate, obsessively driven, and are able to use and undermine the law and the rules for their advantage, like weapons. It is never about the win, never about the money. It is about the kill, the expression of their hatred, about elevating themselves with the suffering of others. Bind, torture, kill. Not only with ropes and knives, but also with power and money, and the subversion of law. Lawlessness is their addiction, their will to power.

When societies become lax and complacent, these sociopaths can possess great political power through great amounts of unprincipled money. And over time they become almost anti-human, destroyers of all that is good, all that is life, all that offends their insatiable sickness with its goodness. They twist the public against itself, and turn a broad sweep of society into their killing grounds. This is the undeniable lesson of the last century. There are monsters, and they walk among us."

Neil Howe has noted in previous articles the catalyst, climax and resolution of Fourth Turnings can be specifically dated. But the degeneracy is more of an era than a date. With only three previous American Fourth Turnings, the regeneracy will probably be a specific event where the American people, faced with growing peril and danger, put aside their differences and rallied around a strong leader to build something new.

In retrospect, the American people were numbed by the Great Depression and the bloody initial battles of the Civil War. They just let FDR and Lincoln do whatever they needed to do. The regeneracy marks a growth in centralized authority and resolute governance at a time of great risk and urgency.

Based upon the reaction of the citizens in the last ten months, the dire problem facing the nation, perceived as the largest threat to our future, happens to be the Deep State establishment currently ruling the country. The captured mainstream media and grey beards running both political parties were completely stunned, horrified, and irate at the unprecedented success achieved by the two anti-establishment candidates, Trump and Sanders.

This election was supposed to follow the script as planned and coordinated by the establishment, with Hillary Clinton defeating Jeb Bush and continuing the corrupt status quo policies agreed to by the bought off leaders of both parties. They badly miscalculated the mood of the country and the whirlwind of change seeking to sweep away the stubborn remnants of a crooked, decrepit, putrid, existing social order. This collective middle finger to the establishment could only happen during a Fourth Turning.

This degeneracy is well under way and is poised to transform and replace the very foundation of this crumbling empire of debt, delusions, and denial. The unanswered question is what happens next. The specific events of a

Fourth Turning are unknowable, but the reaction to those events by the generational cohorts is consistent over time.

We are seeing the reaction of critical thinking Americans as they come to the realization the system is rigged against them. A revolutionary spirit is once again rising among the deplorables.

Based on the current path of this Fourth Turning, this alternating sequence between advancement cycles and atonement cycles is real. The advancement cycles can be seen as establishing, whereas atonement cycles are disestablishing. It is apparent each Fourth Turning alternates between an external struggle and an internal struggle. The American Revolution was a struggle against an external oppressor – Great Britain.

The Civil War was an internal struggle between the industrial North and the agrarian South. The Depression/World War II struggle was mainly against an external threat – Germany, Japan, and Italy. The American Revolution established our country. There was optimism and elation as a new republic, forged under an enlightened Constitution and led by judicious intelligent men, was born. It was clearly an advancement cycle.

The Civil War disestablished states' rights, slavery, agrarian society and Constitutional rights. It was an atonement cycle for our actual and implicit sins. There was no glorious high. The resolution felt more like defeat, with the country exhausted, bitter and angry. The country had exhausted itself, spilling the blood of over one million men. The new High after an atonement cycle is like a cold miserable rainy dark Spring.

The Great Depression/World War II Fourth Turning established a new world order led by the United States. As the only major country left unscathed by the ravages of global war, the U.S. became the producer for the world, whose dollar was unquestioned as the currency of global trade. The new High was unleashed with fanfare and adulation. It was like a delightfully warm Spring, with flowers blooming and children frolicking.

All signs point toward this Fourth Turning being a life or death struggle between the ruling class of sociopathic bankers, corporate elites, and sleazy politicians versus the oppressed and infuriated middle class. The lying, deceit, rigging, deception, theft and other crimes perpetrated by the ruling elites will be atoned for. The heroic patriotic revelations from Edward Snowden, Julian Assange, and Bradley (Chelsea) Manning proving the government and politicians to be lying, corrupt, immoral, sociopathic traitors to the Constitution have undermined the last vestiges of trust in the system and the establishment. The alignment of generational dynamics will provoke the responses to events moving forward. We have been badly led. A silent coup by Deep State perpetrators has led to the complete capture of our economic, financial, judicial and political systems.

A vast swath of the populace has been lured into living beyond their means. The existing system is unsustainable. The Boomer generation does not want to yield on their perceived entitlements. The Millennial generation is saddled with unpayable debts, living in their parents' basements.

Generation X is trapped in the middle of this generational struggle. The huge economic imbalances, created by politicians buying votes and engineering wealth inequality to benefit the few, have built up over decades like flood waters behind a weakening levee. When the levee breaks the morally bankrupt criminal social order will be swept away in the raging torrent to follow.

Winter will eventually turn into Spring, but it might be a bitter, gloomy, austere Spring. Every Fourth Turning brings on forecasts of imminent doom, but that is also a trait of Prophet (Trump, Clinton) Generations. It's how they feel about the prospects of their imminent die off; they expect the entire world to go with them.

The 2008 financial crisis was horrific, scary and an eye opener for those who blindly believed what they were told by their establishment zoo keepers. The regeneracy has begun; trust in the system has further disintegrated; this presidential election has further deepened this distrust of the entrenched establishment; and the coming bust for stocks, bonds, and real estate will knock out the supports for the dwindling remaining trust in this crooked system.

"This might result in a Great Devaluation, a severe drop in the market price of most financial and real assets. This devaluation could be a short but horrific panic, a free-falling price in a market with no buyers. Or it could be a series of downward ratchets linked to political events that sequentially knock the supports out from under the residual popular trust in the system. As assets devalue, trust will further disintegrate, which will cause assets to devalue further, and so on.

Eventually, all of America's lesser problems will combine into one giant problem. The very survival of the society will feel at stake, as leaders lead and people follow. The emergent society may be something better, a nation that sustains its Framers' visions with a robust new pride. Or it may be something unspeakably worse. The Fourth Turning will be a time of glory or ruin." – Strauss & Howe – The Fourth Turning

The next ten or so years will be atonement for decades of bad choices, corrupt leadership, living beyond our means, waging wars of choice across the globe, believing blatant falsehoods, exhibiting willful ignorance, ignoring facts, and failing to uphold the Constitution. Don't think you can escape the consequences of this Fourth Turning. It doesn't matter whether you lived according to a moral code, avoided debt, worked hard, paid taxes, and generally lived an upstanding honorable life.

The death and destruction headed our way will engulf the innocent as well as the guilty. I'm reminded of the penultimate scene in Clint Eastwood's dark, brooding, vengeful western Unforgiven when Little Bill Daggett laments to "killer of women and children" William Munny that he doesn't deserve to die this way. Munny responds, "deserves got nothin' to do with it." Then he pulls the trigger. This is the kind of future we will be dealing with, whether we like it or not.

Globalists Engineer World War III

1780's – The Swedish-Russian War of 1788-1790 began when Swedish troops were intentionally dressed up as Russian troops then sent to attack their own border with Finland, effectively tricking the public into believing Russia had attacked, thereby kicking off a war will killed thousands.

1931 – The Japanese army deliberately destroyed a portion of a Japanese owned railway, then blamed it on Chinese dissidents to justify the military occupation of Manchuria.

1939 – Nazi war engineers dressed up Polish prisoners in Polish military uniforms and directed them to attack a German radio station. They prisoners were shot dead and their bodies left on the scene as evidence of Polish aggression, leading to Hitler's invasion of Poland, signifying the official start of World War II.

1954 – Operation Susannah was an Israeli effort to convince the British military to continue their military presence in the Suez Canal, in support of Israeli interests. Egyptian patsies were hired to detonate bombs in American and British civilian targets, then blamed on the Muslim Brotherhood.

1962 – "In 1962 the US Joint Chiefs of Staff authored a document called Operation Northwoods calling for the US government to stage a series of fake attacks, including the shooting down of military or civilian US aircraft, the destruction of a US ship, sniper attacks in Washington, and other atrocities, to blame on the Cubans as an excuse for launching an invasion. President Kennedy refused to sign off on the plan and was killed in Dallas the next year."

1964 – A U.S. destroyer patrolling the Gulf of Tonkin was attacked by torpedoes, ostensibly by the North Vietnamese, thereby causing President Johnson the authorization of the Gulf of Tonkin Resolution, thus beginning U.S. military involvement in Vietnam. It is now known that no attack actually occurred and that the NSA was involved in fabricating this event.

1967 – "In June 1967 the Israelis attacked the USS Liberty, a US Navy technical research ship, off the coast of Egypt. The ship was strafed relentlessly for hours in an apparent attempt to blame the attack on Egypt and draw the Americans into the Six Day War, but amazingly the crew managed to keep it afloat. In 2007 newly released NSA intercepts confirmed that the Israelis knew they were attacking an American ship, not an Egyptian ship as their cover story has maintained."

1915 – The sinking of the British ocean liner The Lusitania off the coast of Ireland, which was carrying tons of war materials from America, was blamed on German u-boats, leading to a severe diplomatic row which brought the United States into World War I. Speculation remains as to what exactly happened to the Lusitania, however, the official explanation is highly suspicious, and the event was used to achieve the objectives of war financiers to broaden the conflict.

1933 – A German parliamentary building in the Reichstag was set ablaze one month after Hitler's election to the office of Chancellor. It is believed that three Bulgarian communists were to blame, however this is contentious among historians. The event was heavily propagandized by the Nazi party to galvanize support for war.

Are we sleepwalking into World War III, and as events in Syria are shaping up it could come any moment as the biggest October surprise ever. At this stage in the conflict, we are one minor event away from all out war between the world's major super powers, an event which would most certainly result in nuclear war. All that is needed is for the right type of false flag event to serve as provocation.

Imperial Overreach

An analysis of US generals' growing dissatisfaction with the political leadership in Washington sheds new light on the direction in which the American military machine is heading. In particular, it is interesting to observe the military planning for the future of the sea, air, space, cyberspace, and land forces.

At the end of the Cold War, the US armed forces found themselves without any real peer, causing them to gradually alter their strategy and investments in war and conflicts. They transitioned from being a large numerical force geared toward fighting opponents of a similar caliber (the USSR) in accordance with a specific military strategy, to a force focused on hybrid adversaries (regular or militia forces) or foes that were not their equal (Iraq, Syria, Afghanistan, Yugoslavia, and Libya). The US military accordingly proceeded to change its planning and tactics to satisfy the demands of the new tenants in the White House, the notorious Neoconservatives. What resulted was a military doctrine centered on the concept of a unipolar world and aimed at global domination.

Since the early 90s, policy-makers in Washington have had as their objective the utopian goal of global hegemony, and in order to accomplish this the US armed forces had to expand and create new control centers (USAFRICOM, USNORTHCOM), in addition to those already in existence (USEUCOM, USPACOM, USSOUTHCOM, USSOCOM, USSTRATCOM, USTRANSCOM), in every corner of the planet.

This is a typical example of imperial overreach, which has historically been the impetus for the collapse of several kingdoms and empires over the centuries.

The operational capabilities of the US military machine from the 90s to the mid-2000s remained more or less unchanged in every major conflict in which it was involved: Yugoslavia in 1999, Afghanistan in 2001, and Iraq in 2003. These were conflicts in which the defense forces of these nations could not hope to match the attacker's power. Weak air defences were a common denominator for all these nations – a vulnerability that has always been the prerequisite for wars such as those in Iraq and Afghanistan, as well as the US ability to attain air superiority and thus subsequently enjoy unchallenged air space.

Carpet bombing, coupled with the use of staggering numbers of cruise missiles, destroyed the anti-aircraft defenses of both countries, paving the way for massive ground or airborne invasions. One example still fresh in everyone's mind was the intensity of the US strike in the early days of the Iraq war in 2003, which brought unprecedented levels of death and destruction.

Yet despite this advantageous position, the number of dead American and allied soldiers during the years of occupation was enough to shock the American public, perhaps forever changing the perception of the military conflict. The consequences were predictable, with popular pressure forcing a withdrawal of troops from Iraq and a significant reduction of the contingent stationed in Afghanistan.

After a 70-year history of warfare, the old strategy of bombing, invading, and occupying a conquered territory had outlived its usefulness.

The pursuit of a new global strategy required changes. A numerically smaller force was now needed, which would could be deployed on short notice to any corner of the world. US military strategists began to develop plans for new operational training methods and procedures, based on rapid-reaction forces and the ability to reach any theater of war with ease. To this end, US special forces, drones used for reconnaissance and attack, and reliance on the National Reconnaissance Office (NRO) and National Security Agency (NSA) ended up almost totally replacing the previous approach and tactics that had been focused on protecting ground troops.

This organizational change, which allowed the regional command centers a high-degree of strategic and decision-making autonomy, increased the complexity of the American military machine on a devastating scale. The practical results of these transformations could be seen in the control centers' reduced ability to respond to external threats as a single military power under a single flag.

In less than 10 years the United States had gone from a largely ground force able to invade foreign countries with sizable numbers of troops - thanks to its uncontested mastery of the airspace - to an organized military force compartmentalized into small units, which has rarely been asked to intervene directly in a conflict. Thus there has been less emphasis on a search for means and technologies to protect soldiers on the battlefield.

Instead, air power has continued to be the decisive weapon in the war scenarios for several years, especially in North Africa and the Middle East. In 2011 in Libya, one of its latest demonstrations of air superiority, the power of the USAF, combined with that of its allies, provided the necessary cover allowing ground forces (consisting of terrorists who later invaded Syria and the Sinai Peninsula) to conquer and occupy that territory.

To an attentive observer, all these nations that have found themselves in the US military's crosshairs in recent years share a common characteristic, namely a pronounced inability to defend their own airspace. Once the skies were conquered, which provided protection for the troops during ground operations, most of the work was already done.

But this is a formula that has not always had a successful impact on the course of the fighting. Ukraine and Syria are proof, despite representing two very different scenarios.

For entirely different reasons, the two scenarios have highlighted the shortcomings and the strategic and structural weaknesses of the unified military command. In the case of Syria, the air-defense capabilities of the forces loyal to Damascus, rated among the top ten in the world, forced analysts in Washington in 2013 to develop a strategy based on the need to destroy the air-defense systems with the use of numerous cruise missiles that were launched from their fleet in the Mediterranean. Unless the surface-to-air missile (SAM) systems are disabled, the USAF cannot operate with impunity above Syrian skies and risks heavy losses. Syrian anti-aircraft systems are still quite able to neutralize not only an air attack but also a cruise-missile barrage, making any US assault enormously expensive (each Tomahawk costs about a million dollars), counterproductive, and ineffective. This new situation prompted Obama to seek Moscow's help to avoid a conflict that would have caused more than one headache for the Pentagon.

In the case of Ukraine, control of the airspace was uncontested as the Donbass does not possess an air force that can rival that of the Ukrainian military, and thus the military plan was more focused on effective coordination between ground troops, heavy vehicles, and reconnaissance. The goal was to make tactical advances and to conquer the territories in dispute. Yet despite advisors sent from Washington and the technology offered by the United States (the NSA and NRO), Kiev's army suffered from setbacks at the hands of irregular forces far more poorly armed in terms of quality and quantity.

Soon, a series of new situations began to unfold for the United States. Its inability to control the airspace over Syria or gain ground in Ukraine was symptomatic of a deeper malaise affecting the capabilities of the US military and its allies to fight certain battles.

In the minds of US generals and military advisers, these developments were an unprecedented wake-up call. After 70 years of wars and conflicts, the US found itself for the first time in situations where it could neither afford the luxury of intervening directly (Ukraine) nor be able to provide a concrete solution that would reverse the situation on the battlefield (Syria). This was a cause for concern, forcing American political leaders to rethink their entire approach to military confrontation and to formulate a new strategy to face these new challenges.

In some public meetings conducted by General Robert Neller (Commandant of the Marine Corps) and General Joseph Dunford (Chairman of the Joint Chiefs of Staff), both men have highlighted the most important challenge for the future of the United States military. They foresee a transformation, over just 15 years, into a military force capable of fighting not only enemies that are well equipped (as in Syria and Ukraine) but also on par with the US (Russia and China). It is a revolution, or more precisely, a return to the past.

In defining these challenges, Dunford spoke of what is referred to in military jargon as the "4+1," i.e., the nations that the US Strategic Command sees as posing major challenges over the next 10 years, in other words: Russia, China, North Korea, and Iran + Terrorism. In describing this approach, Dunford has outlined a future war scenario mainly involving short-, medium-, and long-range ballistic missiles (SRBMs, MRBMs, and ICBMs, respectively), anti-ballistic systems (ABMs), cyber attacks, and the ability to deny access or airspace (A2/AD).

What will surprise the reader is the admission by Neller and Dunford that the United States has some operational issues that could easily be exploited by opponents. Rival countries (peer competitors) have made technological strides in the past decade allowing them to almost close the gap with the US military in vital sectors for future war scenarios in many fields, such as the following:

• Fifth-generation aircraft (J-31 and PAK FA) with stealth capabilities.

• Long-range ballistic missiles (R-36M) and short-/medium-range missiles (Iskander).

• ICBMs with supersonic speed (unable to be intercepted by current and future ABMs).

• The ability to produce cybernetic damage with real-world effects.

• Increasingly advanced technology to deny airspace to an opponent either electronically (EW) or mechanically (S-300, S-400, S-500).

In all these challenges we can see America's advantages being diminished. Another worrying aspect, of which both commanders are aware, is the need to have an Internet/intranet connection in order to operate at full capacity. The interconnection between men and means for the United States is a force multiplier, just as is the need to project power on enemy shores through naval forces. Strategies to deny these advantages are essential components of Russia's and China's military doctrines.

The new generation of anti-ship missiles (DF-26, BrahMos II, Qader and P-900) offer a clear example of how Beijing and Moscow are reacting to the steady degradation of the frameworks for global peace. If the US Navy is denied a radius of several hundred kilometers, which is needed in order to control ships and aircraft carriers close to an enemy coast, this is a big problem for American military planners. The anti-ship missiles also offer an economic advantage: they cost little but can sink ships worth billions of dollars. They are thus ideal for challenging the US Navy, whose unparalleled power can be seen in its 10 aircraft carriers. Furthering this strategy, Russia and China are working on beyond-visual-range (BVR) missiles that, combined with stealth aircraft (J-20 and PAK FA), can deny the United States the essential ability to anticipate a lethal attack on its aircraft carriers that can be launched from a safe distance.

The goal for Beijing, Moscow, or Tehran is always the same: to keep Washington from being able to approach their shores or operate in international waters, in order to prevent the huge American aircraft carriers from being used as a launch pad for military operations.

In terms of strategic security, the protection of the skies is the first priority for any military planner. ABM systems, like Chinese or Russian S-300, S-400, and S-500s, are, as stated, designed with the goal of creating an impenetrable airspace for ICBMs and/or fourth- or fifth-generation stealth aircraft. Without air cover and naval platforms, the functional capabilities of any ground troops are drastically reduced. Add to this SRBMs such as Iskander missiles, which can wipe out whole platoons, and one can easily understand why Dunford is worried that he has already lost his technological and operational edge when faced with a competitor of similar stature.

Certainly the evolution of the American military-industrial complex (MIC) has not facilitated the task of the strategists at the Pentagon. Programs such as the F-35 (fifth-generation stealth aircraft) that were supposed to compete with equivalent Sino-Russian projects have been beset by numerous problems and massive cost overruns, probably the result of a widespread system of corruption, leaving the United States at a disadvantage in future contests for air supremacy.

Even the US nuclear arsenal (nuclear triad) could use some upgrades to keep it on par with Russia's, and those modernizations are estimated to cost about a trillion dollars over 10 years, a figure the US Treasury does not currently possess (without printing extra money, but that's another story). Recently Moscow conducted a long list of tests of its ballistic missiles that are capable of achieving unprecedented speed (Mach 6-7), able to change direction after launch, and which possess a significantly increased operating range (17,000 kms), making all current and future anti-ballistic systems ineffective and useless.

Losing the Edge

Moscow and Beijing have practical considerations (but which are, in a way, almost philosophical) based on the enormous difference in their military spending compared to Washington. This has forced them to aim for inexpensive systems that are nevertheless just as effective.

A perfect example, already fully operational, is the development and use of Kalibr missiles - the Russian response to the US cruise missile. Similar to the American version, its main difference is that it can be fired from small ships. To understand Washington's level of anxiety, one need only analyze its reaction to the Black Sea launch of the first Kalibr missiles in 2015 toward targets in Syria. The Pentagon declared its surprise at Russia's "new" ability to launch such missiles at a distance of thousands of kilometers from such small ships (with consequently reduced costs). This inability to recognize an opponent's capabilities is perhaps symptomatic of underlying problems.

The Kalibr missiles allowed Moscow to gain a tactical advantage, which, according to US military advisers, changed the strategic balance in the Middle East. This was enough to dramatically reduce one of the US's largest advantages: cruise missiles. Top US advisors panicked, realizing they needed to immediately offer an adequate response to this new situation. Moreover, the strategy of equipping small ships with Kalibr missiles has allowed Moscow to produce a large number of corvettes, vastly expanding the total power of the Russian fleet. Moscow currently has quite a number of these ships, all armed in this way.

The United States prefers the opposite philosophical stance in terms of its projects. Long-term projects are being promoted that offer massive opportunities for price gouging and extra profits for contractors and brokers: stealth ships (USS Zumwalt), mega carriers (Gerald R. Ford class), and the F-35 are just a few examples. Without offering any immediate technological advances, especially in relation to the countermoves of the "4 + 1," it seems that this is where the modernization efforts of the US armed forces are focused.

Paradoxically, although the US cannot even deploy a few F-35s, nations such as North Korea and Iran already have strategies in place to use deterrence to nullify the current American operational supremacy. In this sense, despite sanctions and the international climate of hostility, Pyongyang has managed to produce a submarine equipped with nuclear SLBMs – a big step forward that greatly expands its ability to deter the United States and South Korea. In Iran, the mass production of domestically developed weapons (Bavar-373) similar to the S-300 system (and just as effective) have been designed to deny any operational capacity over the skies of the Islamic Republic and its allies (Hezbollah and Syria) in the immediate future.

Washington is asking its generals to be prepared for a large-scale conflict with opponents of a stature equal to its own, but the reality behind the scenes is troubling, and the desperate cries of Dunford and Neller, appropriately kept hidden from the media, offer proof of this. Just a simple comparison of the military doctrines of China, Russia, and the United States – in regard to their long-term trajectory - shows that Washington, although possessing a numerical advantage in terms of the forces and means at its disposal, lacks the necessary capability to properly unify the powerful components of the US military in order to dominate its rivals.

This is probably why General Dunford said recently that subsequent strategic plans by US armed forces will not be made public. Evidently, hiding these endemic weaknesses is necessary to avoid jeopardizing a cornerstone of the strategy of US forces: the ability to project power and intimidate opponents without having to take real action.

Conclusion

Because they have effectively taken advantage of all the above factors, Russia, Iran, and their allies have attained the necessary skills to prevent direct US intervention in various contexts, from Ukraine to Syria.

In analyzing what has not worked in the Middle East or Eastern Europe, the US is blinded by the complexity of its military system and is focusing mostly on its inability to rapidly devise a workable strategy that is inexpensive in terms of human casualties. This is the main reason Washington has been forced to lean on outside actors to influence events on the ground (mercenary battalions in Ukraine and Salafis and Wahhabis in Syria). As we can see, these are all choices that do not pay off in the long run, instead allowing other rising powers to dominate the United States without necessarily resorting to a direct confrontation.

The wars of the third millennium AD also heavily rely on psychological factors and deterrence, as well as the essential ability to influence an opponent with false information. Take the example of Syria and the Russian intervention. No one at the Pentagon or CIA was able to predict Russia's air and naval deployment, which was accomplished in less than 48 hours. No one, least of all Dunford, was ready at the time with a well-defined plan to respond to this move. In addition to technical and organizational inefficiencies, there is a clearly inadequate ability to decipher an opponent's moves such as one does in chess. The ability to catch an opponent off guard has already proved its effectiveness in the conflict in Ukraine, in which Crimea was reunified with Russia without a shot being fired and with full popular support.

Dunford and Neller have grasped that any future battlefield will be a hostile environment in terms of air superiority, Internet connectivity, and the simultaneous management of resources across a broad geographical spectrum. It is a challenge with - by the general's own admission - a far from obvious outcome. Washington's policy, which is dominated by lobbies and corruption, requires an unprecedented turnaround in its military apparatus. But this is what is needed in order to meet the future challenges of a multipolar world with different nations (allied together) with capabilities equal to that of the US military machine.

The truth, which is difficult for US policymakers to accept, is that the current environment of the military-industrial complex (MIC) leaves little room to maneuver, given the gargantuan projects that are in place. The F-35 is unlikely to be put on hold while the project is completely revised and its actual ability to carry out the tasks required of a fifth-generation fighter reviewed. The same could be said about the development of expensive ships such as the USS Enterprise and USS Zumwalt, in which several hundred billion dollars have already been invested.

Military spending is an essential gear in the machine of the US system of oligarchy, but the consequences are starting to drag down the future military capabilities of the United States. Its rivals are catching up, using systems that are more advanced, more economical, and more effective, while also easier to use or replicate. The military leaders at the Pentagon are starting to show telling signs of impatience, calling for a transformation that will be difficult to achieve, since it will require a sea change in the country's top-brass establishment. The ultimate consequences are evidence of a pattern that is slowly draining Washington's wallet and greatly reducing the competitive advantage that Washington possesses.

Now, with the World War 3 calls getting louder, the US and China have deployed a code reminiscent of a system used during the Cold War that will hopefully help both sides avoid a "miscalculation" as the two countries are now expected to "meet more often."

Meanwhile, the Pentagon says China is "rapidly closing the gap" between itself and the US in terms of air and space capabilities.

Power Projections

China aims to boost its maritime forces, but it already has an edge over its rivals in terms of the sheer size of its air and naval fleets.

	China	Japan	U.S. Carrier Strike Group	Vietnam	Philippines
Aircraft carriers • = 1	1	0	1	0	0
Destroyers/ frigates • = 1	73	47	9	7	3
Submarines • = 1	58	16	0 to 2	0	0
Fighter/ bomber aircraft • = 10	2,100	353	54	217	8

Sources: U.S. Department of Defense, World Air Forces 2015 report, Japan Self-Defense Force (Japan fighter)

Gates of Vienna

"The long-term goal of the Jihad Generation is to destroy Europe through civil war and then build an Islamic society from the ashes..." warns Professor Gilles Kepel, who is a specialist on Islamic and contemporary Arab world. Decades ago, Europe's leaders adopted a general policy of "openness" to the Islamic world in general, and the Arab world in particular. They decided to welcome migrants from the Muslim world by hundreds of thousands but without asking them to integrate. They made cultural relativism and multiculturalism their guiding principles. They acted as if Islam could mingle in the Western world harmoniously and without difficulty. Europe's leaders disseminated the idea that the West was guilty of oppressing Muslims and had to pay for its sins. They therefore sowed the seeds of anti-Western resentment among Muslims in Europe.

When in the Muslim world jihadis started to kill, Europe's leaders wanted to believe that the attacks would take place in the Muslim world only. They thought that by not interfering with what European jihadis were planning, they would not risk jihadi attacks on European soil.

When Jews were attacked, Europe's leaders decided that the problem was not jihad, but Israel. They stressed the need not to "export Middle East conflict in Europe." Hoping to please followers of radical Islam and show them Europe could understand their "grievances," they placed increasing pressure on Israel. They also increased their financial and political support for the "Palestinian cause."

When Europeans were attacked, they did not understand why. They had done their best to please the Muslims. They had not even harassed the jihadists. They still do not know how to react.

Many of them now say privately what they will never say in public: it is probably too late.

There are six to eight million Muslims in France, and more than thirty million in Western Europe. Hundreds of jihadis are trained and ready to act -- anytime, anyplace. European intelligence services know that they want to make "dirty bombs." Surveys show that tens of thousands of Muslims living in Europe approve of jihadi attacks in Europe. Millions of Muslims living in Europe keep silent, behave as if they see nothing and hear nothing, and protest only when they think they have to defend Islam.

European political leaders know that every decision they make may provoke reactions among the Muslims living in Europe. Muslim votes matter. Riots occur easily. In France, Belgium, other European countries,

Islamists are present in the army and police forces. In the meantime, Islamist organizations recruit and Islamic lobbies gain ground.

European governments are now hostages. The European media are also hostages.

In most European countries, "Islamophobia" is considered a crime -- and any criticism of Islam may be considered "Islamophobic." People trying to warn Europe, such as the Dutch MP Geert Wilders, despite an apparently biased judge and forged documents against him, are now on trial.

Books on radical Islam are still published but surrounded by silence. Books praising the glory of Islam are in every bookstore. When Bat Ye'or's Eurabia was published in Europe, she was denounced and received hundreds of death threats. Bruce Bawer While Europe Slept, published in the U.S., was not even available in Europe. Ten years later, the situation is worse.

Political movements expressing anger and concerns are rising. All are demonized by political power holders and the media. They have almost no chance of gaining more influence.

Populations are gnawed by fear, frustration and impotence. They are looking for answers, but cannot find them. A few hours after the attacks on Brussels, a man on Belgian television said that Europe is on the verge of suicide.

Europe looks like a dying civilization. European governments created a situation that can only lead to more attacks, more massacres, and maybe unspeakable disasters. Europe's leaders continue to react with speeches and a few police operations.

If some European governments decided to restore their abolished borders, it could take years, and most European leaders would probably disagree with such a policy. Meanwhile, millions more "migrants" will enter Europe, and among them many more jihadis. In spite of the mayhem created in Germany by "migrants" who arrived in 2015, Angela Merkel said she would not change her decisions. No Western European government dared to disagree with her, except Viktor Orbán in Hungary, a lone voice of dissent.

In Brussels, as in Paris earlier, people gathered where the attacks took place. They brought candles and flowers to mourn the victims. They sang sentimental songs. They cried. There were no shouts of revolt against jihad. Members of the Belgian government called on the Belgian people to avoid reactions of violence, and declared that Muslims are the main victims of terrorism.

In Europe's near future, more people will bring candles, flowers and songs to mourn victims. Another two or three jihadists will be arrested. But nothing will be done.

Pakistan: A Cancer to the World

There was a time when a young Mujahideen commander named Osama bin Laden was a core ally of the US in the fight against Soviet communism and central planning. Well, that particular affair did not end too well for either Osama, nor for the USSR (although one may argue that "communism and central planning" are experiencing a second renaissance courtesy of capitalist central banking). Along the same lines, Pakistan which as recently as 3 weeks ago was considered a core US ally, has very promptly fallen out of favor following the death of that other abovementioned former ally. Yet Pakistan is not wasting time. Two days after Pakistani PM Yousuf Raza Gilani took a direct stab at deteriorating US-Paki relations by saying that China is now his country's "best friend", China has retorted in kind by announcing it will provide another 50 JF-17 fighter jets to Pakistan on an "expedited" basis. The WSJ reports that "the agreement to accelerate supply of the jointly developed jets, the first 50 of which are being assembled in Pakistan, came as Pakistan's Prime Minister Yusuf Raza Gilani held talks in Beijing during a visit that he has used to portray China as an alternative source of military and civilian aid. "We're getting the 50 jets, on top of the ones we already have. Something has been agreed in Beijing, so they'll be expedited" he said." In other words: step aside US, here comes China. As for those billions in USD aid which somehow never ended up being used to buy US Treasuries (Pakistan is nowhere in the listing of US Treasury holders), it is now clear into whose pocket they are going (at $15 million a pop, those are big pockets). Lastly, this is more than just posturing by China: the country is clearly indicating its latest and greatest sphere of influence. As a reminder, "It was reported in 2008 that Azerbaijan and Zimbabwe had placed orders for the aircraft and nine other countries, including Bangladesh, Myanmar, Egypt, Iran, Lebanon, Malaysia, Morocco, Nigeria, Sri Lanka and Algeria were showing interest."

China is Pakistan's biggest arms supplier and its third-biggest trading partner.

The JF-17 is a potent symbol of the two countries' friendship, and a key part of Pakistan's plans to upgrade its aging fleet of American-supplied F-16s and French-made Mirages and to try to match the air power of neighboring India—its arch rival.

The U.S. has repeatedly delayed delivery of F-16s to Pakistan, and has insisted that they not be used against India, with which Washington is now cultivating a strategic partnership to counterbalance Beijing's clout in Asia.

China and Pakistan began developing the relatively cheap multipurpose fighter in 1999 and Pakistan, which has said it wants 250 of them altogether, inducted its first squadron of JF-17s last year, and a second earlier this year.

The air-force spokesman said he did not know whether the second batch of 50 jets would be assembled in Pakistan or delivered whole from China.

He also declined to discuss whether they would be the basic so-called Block I models, like the first batch, or an upgraded Block II version, which military aviation experts say could include radar-evading stealth technology—potentially giving Pakistan that capability for the first time.

Questions also remain over the new jets' engines. The first batch were all fitted with Russian ones, but Russian officials have expressed reservations about supplying more of those engines as Pakistan and China have been marketing the JF-17 in many of Russia's traditional markets.

The Starting Point

In a show of force dubbed "The Power of Velayat" (a nod to the Republic's religious doctrine), Iran tested what looked like several medium-range Qiam-1s, missiles based on the Shahab of which Iran has hundreds stashed in underground storage facilities.

"Defensive" or no, the tests obviously fly in the face of western sanctions and underscore the extent to which Tehran deeply mistrusts its regional rivals in Israel and Saudi Arabia.

"Iran's Islamic Revolutionary Guards Corps (IRGC) test-fired two ballistic missiles on Wednesday morning that it said were designed to be able to hit Israel, defying a threat of new sanctions from the United States," Reuters reports. "The IRGC fired two Qadr missiles from northern Iran which hit targets in the southeast of the country 1,400 kms (870 miles) away, Iranian agencies said. The nearest point in Iran is around 1,000 km from Tel Aviv and Jerusalem."

In a testament to the "success" of Washington's foreign policy towards Iran, Brigadier General Hossein Salami, deputy commander of the IRGC said the following: "The missiles fired today are the results of sanctions. The sanctions helped Iran develop its missile program."

The world is finally awakening to the fact that World War III

has begun in earnest; that the Islamic World and the Judeo-Christian world are now truly at war.